The Tragedy Of Losing You

by T.R. Weiss

Chapter One

Having

Having You

having you
felt like
i had found
the other half
of my heart
and nothing could separate us
now that we had fought through life
to find each other

but time drove a wedge
between us
and we are separated once more

this is the tragedy
of losing you

Ghost Of Our Love

i looked into that antique shop
that we once spent several hours in
one brisk fall day
and my heart sank in my chest
for it was just another place
i could never go to again
because it is cursed with the ghost
of our love

the feeling of having you
was like nothing
i had ever experienced before

it was as if the universe
had suddenly tipped the scales
in my favor
and everything was right in the world

our love could have built cities
traversed deserts
and climbed mountains

i remember you once told me
that human beings look for things
in their lovers
that they wish they had
themselves

i always wondered
what you saw in me
and what i could've changed
to make you stay

together
we were the
king and queen
of rebels and lovers

together
we were conquerers

in all honesty
although things ended badly
i don't regret
a single moment
we spent together

i would be fooling myself
if i didn't admit
that every word i write
is a cry into the void
begging fate
to bring you back to me

something about us
just seemed so right
from the very start

these mere photographs
could never contain
our love

and no book of any length
could ever describe
how i feel about you

if you asked me
to fly to the moon
and bring it back down to you

i would do it
in a heartbeat

your love
made me feel
like i could do the impossible

we knew it was a long shot

we knew the odds
weren't in our favor
and we knew that things
might not work out

but we decided
to give it a try
anyway

and i will never regret that.

things were thrown
broken mirrors
bad luck

it's no wonder
it had to end

though i know i can never have you again
my heart still aches in my chest
for it knows that you are out there
and it can never understand
though i try to explain
with oh so many words

the heart only understands love
and does not understand
all of the reasons
it had to end...

we met on my first day
working at the diner on 4th avenue
we got high together after work
and just that taste
of you
was enough
to make me

an addict.

i have always been jealous.

jealous that somehow
somebody
could love you
in ways i never could

i am afraid that someone
might deserve you
far more than i ever could

perhaps that makes me selfish...

it wasn't easy.

nothing about us
was easy

but we didn't mind

we didn't sign up for easy
we signed up for a flip of a coin
a moment of chance
together, you and i
we dared to dream.

there is nothing in the world
that hurts quite as much
as having loved someone
with all of your heart
and then having
to let them go

i cannot keep count
of all the times
i have cried for you

i am afraid to sleep
each night i lay awake in bed
for fear that i might dream of you
and the process
of getting over you
would start all over again...

what i miss the most
about you
was the feeling of your body
next to mine
wrapped in the same soft blankets
cuddling without a care
and making love into the early morning

i could never decide
to believe your sober words
or your drunk words

in hindsight
perhaps inebriation
was an unexpected fortune teller

you didn't break me.

i broke myself
by tying my heartstrings
to you
and believing that you
would hesitate
before pulling me apart
and leaving me desolate

every kiss
every hug
every gaze
every smile

it all felt
like christmas morning
as a small child

you were the greatest gift
life ever gave me

Chapter Two

Losing

you asked me
if i wanted
to see other people

of course i didn't
but i didn't want you
to think i was clingy
or something like that

i should have stood up
for what i wanted
when i had the chance

you were the only one
who loved me
without wanting
something in return

you made my heart feel
so full
of love and light

i wish that our ending
could have been better

our story deserved a sunset
to match the beauty of its sunrise

and its a shame
we never got that.

it hurts me to think
that perhaps
we just aren't meant for each other
and we won't be
reunited
one day

my attraction to you
felt so complete

it was
spiritual
physical
emotional

and now
without you
i just feel empty.

losing you
was the hardest thing
i have ever had
to go through

i wish i could go back
to all those late nights
strolling through the city
just talking about everything
together

the worst part
about losing you
was losing
the part of myself
that loved you

sometimes it feels so hard
just to live another day
just to take another breath

sometimes it feels so hard
just to keep going

without you
even sunny days
may as well be cloudy

some day
i am going to build up a courage
to tell a therapist
all about us
and about you

but i'm afraid
that by hearing about you
they might find themselves
irresistibly attracted
to you as well

you should have seen
the look in my eyes
of pure joy and excitement
the first time
i told anyone
we were together

and the look
of heartbreaking devastation
when i had to tell someone
for the first time
that we were separated...

i will never forget the way
you encouraged me
to follow me dreams
and express myself
through art

everyone always talks about
how great it is
to date your best friend

but they never seem to mention
how devastating it is
to lose your best friend
and lover
at the same time
when it ends

the days seem to last forever
as i ruminate over heartbreak
the minutes tick by endlessly

and even when
i make it
through the day
i can't sleep at night

truly, you haunt
my every hour

i just can't seem
to keep my mind
off of you

we walked through the fields
running our hands
through the wheat

it felt so natural
and us, connected
to each other
and everything

i wonder
if i shall ever tire
of writing about you

perhaps i shall
on the day
that i am finally able
to stop thinking about you

writing
is my greatest release
and my greatest prison

it's so hard to be the light
in someone else's life
when internally
you're bleeding and dying
trying so hard
just to make it
through the night

you held me
like i was the only thing
keeping you
on the face of the earth
and if you stopped holding me
you might drift off
into outer space

it's so easy
to let life
pass you by
while you're stuck
remembering
better days

making love to you
felt like
the fulfillment
of everything i wanted
in love

love and lust
passions collide
you and i

perfection.

i miss the times
we spent together
more than i miss
anything
or anyone
else

the moment stretched on
into infinity

you asking me
if we should end it

i broke every rule
for you

and yet you
would not lift a finger
for me

i can't even look
at the color blue
anymore

without feeling sad
remembering
how it was
your favorite color

<u>Chapter Three</u>

Wishing

wishing on a star
begging to re-live
all of our moments
again

as if
for the first time

if leaving was easy
you never really loved them
in the first place

perhaps only the grave
will cure the longing
i feel for you
deep within my heart

i wish that i had told you
more often
how i felt

the good and the bad

communication is the most important part
of any relationship
and yet
it is so underrated
in our society

we may not have been
romeo and juliet
but what we had
was special
and it mattered
to me

i wish that i could write music
so that i
could've written you
love songs
when we were together
and songs of heartbreak
after we broke up

innocence
teaches us
to take the risks

but experience
teaches us
that sometimes
the risk
is not worth
the reward

there was nothing calm about us.

we were a storm
a raging hurricane
a ship
in constant threat
of sinking

but i am proud
of what we built
together
even
if it wasn't
perfect

in your touch
i found
a thousand emotions
from excitement
to lust
to fear of loss

the quietist people
hold the deepest secrets

i watched you
move across the room
and i swear
if that
had been
the first time
i ever saw you

it would've been
love at first sight
each and every time

the worst tragedy in the world
is when two people
who love each other
oh so much

just can't
make it work

i woke up from a nightmare
and instinctively
i reached over
to your side
of the bed
seeking comfort

but i grasped
only empty space
and with a rush to the head
i remembered
that the nightmare
was nothing
compared to the reality
of losing you

your lips

oh, the things
the many things
they can do

against my better judgement
drunk, at three in the morning
i called you over
and we
reclaimed our passion
as if we
had never broken up

but in the morning
i realized
we had merely reheated
old leftovers
that had long since gone bad

but i didn't realize that
until it was too late

our love ended

the birds still chirped
the sun still shone
the earth still spun

it all felt wrong.

how could anything
continue on
after it felt
like my world
had ended?

i wish
i could take back
all those times
i told you
i was sorry
and said
it was all my fault
just so i
could keep you
for a little while longer

all that time
i was trying so hard
to save something
that was already dead

electricity
up and down
my spine

flowing
from my lips
to other places
as the night goes on

in my right mind
i see all the reasons
why we
had to end

but the moment
i see you
and look into your eyes

all my reason melts away
and all i have left
is desolate desire

i can't stop wanting you
even though you
are not right
for me

you always seemed to think
that you could kiss away
our problems
and for a while
i let you believe that

but all things
come back
in the end

and band-aids
wont heal
a gaping wound

i can't pretend
that i
was blameless
in what happened

but until you accept
your part in it

i just can't
admit
mine

what am i supposed to do now
that we
are no longer together
and i am left
with the memories
of you
showing me
the house you grew up in
in some small, faraway town

the details of the stories
your grandmother
used to tell you
and a thousand memories
of our time together

i feel as if i have the keys
to a beautiful mansion
that has long since burned down
leaving me with nothing
but pain

Chapter Four

Healing

how resilient
is the human heart
that breaks
a thousand times
and yet
it still
somehow
pieces itself
back together
every time

our memories
may fade away
like old polaroids

but i
will never forget
the way
you made
me feel

forgiving
is
the ultimate
revenge

i find anything i can
to distract myself
whenever thoughts of you
begin to surface

the news
a movie
music

anything, anything
to keep my mind
off of you

it seems as if
every day
the news
gets more and more
depressing
and my hope
for the future
gets dimmer
and dimmer

there are marches in the streets
turmoil in every town
it feels
as if
a change
is about to happen

even when hope
begins to dim
it can be
reignited
when we examine
the things
in life
that are positive
and full of joy

the great challenge
of being alive
is learning the truth
about things
without giving up
that they
can ever
be changed

our times
are defined
by polarization
and discord

i wish that we all
could find common ground
and not feel
so disjointed

there is nothing like
the morning sun
to breathe some light
into the soul

even a broken heart
still beats
and that
is the magic
of the human spirit

how many
one night stands
will it take
to forget
the countless
perfect nights
we had together?

i look at the clouds
and see
shapes of us
together

our dates
our fights
our time

but i shake it away
for thinking
about you
does me
no good

breathe in.

breathe out.

think about nothing.

meditate.

perhaps
this is the only way
i can free my mind
of your chains

even if
our time together
didn't end well
that doesn't mean
that our good memories
together
don't mean something to me

they do

but deep down inside
i wish
i could pretend
they didn't

the clocks tick a little faster now
time doesn't stretch quite as far

and at last
things aren't
quite as bad
as they used to be

even a stopped clock
is right twice a day
and sometimes a bad relationship
is occasionally good

the hard truth
of the matter
is that we see
these good moments
and think
that if we tried hard enough
we could fix our lovers
and make them treat us
right all the time

but these good moments
are not the potential
of bad relationships

they are mere chance
and though it is difficult
we have to let go
of things
that have no chance
of working out

writing
is bleeding out
through the ink
of a pen

perhaps
if i drive
far enough
and for enough time

i will eclipse the radius
of the power of our memories

there is nothing
quite as devastating
as finding something
in your room
that was left there
by someone
you once loved

even
in the longest
of the darkest
of nights

the rise of the sun
in the morning
is always guaranteed

some time has passed
and finally
i have started to feel
that my heart
no longer aches
to be reunited with you
and i can breathe
without feeling
like my life
is over
without you

ABOUT THIS BOOK

"The Tragedy of Losing You" is a poetry collection about love, loss, and heartbreak. It is about the feeling of losing someone who means the world to you and the life of someone with a broken heart— and the eventual healing every broken heart finds through the passage of time.

17417577R00068

Made in the USA
Middletown, DE
27 November 2018